S **SKILLS SPECIFIC**

I **INDUCTION**

M **MODULE**

Maple Leaf Publishing Inc.
Alberta Canada

Skill Based Project
Copyright © 2020 **NAURIN KHERAJ**

All rights reserved. No part of this book may be reproduced or transmitted in any form or by any means, electronic or mechanical, including photocopying, recording, or by any information storage and retrieval system, without written permission of the publisher.

Paperback: **978-1-77419-019-7**
E-book: **978-1-77419-030-2**
Rev. Date: **07 31, 2020**

MAPLE LEAF PUBLISHING INC.
3rd Floor 4915 54 St Red Deer,
Alberta T4N 2G7 Canada

General Inquiries & Customer Service
Phone: +1 (403) 356-0255
Toll Free: 1-(888)-498-9380
Email: info@mapleleafpublishinginc.com

To My Mother

Who has shared in all my joys and sorrows,
my trials, failures, and achievement;
and whose love, courage,
and devotion have been the strength of my striving,
this book is affectionately dedicated to my mum.

Love you always Mom!!!!!

Introduction

Skills Specific Induction Module is developed for students of any age who engage with different curriculum for the first time. This, on the first hand, will enhance essential skills that are considered necessary to explore and understand and approach the curriculum. These skills include students' involvement in reflective practices, critical thinking, language, literacy, and social skills. The module will give students exposure to these skills and will promote their active engagement in learning and practicing those skills through various classroom experiences.

Rationale:

The need for Skill Specific Module is to encourage students to be reflective of their selves and develop an understanding that they will be using in various skills and competencies. The Module aims to involve students in different classroom exercises aimed at developing critical thinking, reflective practices, social competence, and language, and literacy skills. students will be therefore engaged to:

- Work collaboratively and independently on tasks, assignments, and activities.
- Read, analyze and synthesize information provided in the module.
- Discuss and debate issues in pairs, small groups, and with the whole class.
- Use appropriate communication skills to participate in discussion and othe group activities.
- Articulate ideas in written and oral form
- Present information to communicate ideas in a coherent and compelling manner
- Examine an issue or a topic from multiple perspectives
- Ask relevant questions to clarify and extend learning

Module Approach:

The Handbook puts forward fifteen one-day strategies that aim to enhance students' skills and competencies, as highlighted above by involving them in the overall learning process. Strategies and approaches are developed, compiled, and adapted from various sources to integrate the core skills with students learning throughout the module.

Handbook Design:

The handbook includes 15 labeled and organized strategies for each day of the class that students will participate in throughout 8-week. Each strategy contains the following:

- Activity Title
- Inspiring Quote
- Instructions

- Instructions
- Sample Response
- Classroom Tips
- Worksheet template
- Additional resource (if any)

Expectations from Students:
Students are expected to participate in learning and applying critical and reflective thinking, language, literacy, social, and interpersonal skills each day as the module progresses. Strategies are designed in a way that not only introduces an ability but involves students in practicing those skills through an integrated approach.

At the end of each day, students are expected to:

- Learn or enhance skills through various strategies
- Practice skills through teacher facilitation
- Participate in group and independent learning activities
- Build capacity to think critically and reflect on their learning process
- Finish their day with a written reflection using personalization or creative writing promt
- Organize and manage classwork and activity worksheets in their portfolios

Specific Skills explained

Reflective Thinking:

A reflection is a form of personal response to experiences, situations, events, or new information. It is a critical thinking and learning phase where each experience, circumstance, event, or further information is analyzed in a way that learners can make meaning out of it. There is neither a right nor a wrong way of reflective thinking; there are just questions to explore and attempts to respond to them in meaningful way[1].

Critical Thinking:

Critical thinking is that mode of thinking – about any subject, content or problem – in which the thinker improves the quality of his or her thinking by skillfully taking charge of the structures inherent in thinking and imposing intellectual standards upon them[2]. It involves following competences:

- Identify elements in a reasoned case
- Clarify and interpret concepts
- Conclude meanings from the claims
- Evaluate arguments and present your own
- Analyze, evaluate and make connections
- Produce your arguments

Language and Literacy Skills:

Language skills involve reading, writing, speaking, and listening, which requires cognition and articulation of thoughts that enhance communication between people. To interact with the world around them, to present their ideas creatively, and to understand various perspective, this language, and literacy skills are crucial. 'Literacy focuses on developing each child's ability to understand and use language as an integral part of learning in all areas[3]'.

Social Competence:

Social competence in children includes effective use of all the skill set required to be better able to adapt to people and changing situations. These skills include social, language, cognitive, and emotional skills. It involves knowledge and skills children need to achieve their goals in a way that enable them to use these skills effectively when interacting with others. Being socially competent, thus means to be able to respond to conflicts positively and cooperatively and engage in discussion in a constructively[4].

Index

S. No	Title and Objectives	Pg.
1	**Learning Explored** To let students know each other better. To involve students in thinking about learning and how it is occurred. To encourage them to reflect on their own learning practices.	7
2	**A Story from Literature** To introduce reflective thinking model through the video "Given Tree" To engage students in practicing reflective thinking skills using ordinary objects	8
3	**I am Human Nation** To dig into students prior understanding about brain and its functions To facilitate students in thinking about thinking To build a con structive view about thinking	9
4	**Most Precious Gift from God** To make students aware of passing time and it use To identify various ways time is spend in our everyday lives To encourage students to think about ways in which time can be used constructively	11
5	**Reading Pictures** To encourage students to analyze events and ideas critically To facilitate them negotiating and sharing their respective ideas constructively with others	12
6	**Steadfastness on Beliefs** To recognize the strength of group pressure To learn to work as team To encourage students to remain focused and steadfast on their decisions	14
7	**My Actions My world** To encourage students to analyze events, ideas and their own actions critically To make them aware of various choices and their possible consequences To facilitate them negotiating and sharing their respective ideas constructively with others	15

8	**Story Sketch** To facilitate students in learning close reading technique To involve students in analyzing text and making connections through visualization	17
9	**Human Squares** To encourage them to work in teams To determine significance of individual efforts in developing a successful team To assist them in planning and managing resources (material and human)	22
10	**Meaning Making** To facilitate students in learning close reading technique To involve students in analyzing text and making connections	23
11	**The Next Stop** To enhance students visual learning skill through predictions To involve students in analyzing text and making connections through video	26
12	**Intellect In Action** To enhance students critical inquiry through text To involve students in close reading technique To encourage them to share and learn from each other	27
13	**My Unique Perspective** To enhance students critical thinking skills To encourage them to think and analyze various perspectives to make connections and derive meaning	32
14	**Informed Decisions** To encourage them to think and analyze various perspectives to make connections and derive meaning To facilitate them in making conscious decisions	33
15	**The Final Day** To involve students in creative expressions of their learning throughout the term To encourage them to reflect on their own learning and assess their own progress.	34

LEARNING EXPLORED

Start the skill based module for students with an icebreaking activity. **First**, ask students to pick or think silently about
- An object that they see on their study table *or*
- Any object that they want to keep on their imaginary study table *or*
- Any object they like to keep with them while they study.

> 'Looking around with stars in your eyes and amazement at the tools that are available to you can inspire generosity and creativity and connection."
>
> Seth Godin

Now, divide students in groups around empty tables in the classroom and instruct them to introduce or share their selected objects to the group. Students will be introducing themselves as objects on the table keeping in mind the following guidelines.
- What is the object? What purpose does it serve?
- How does it aid in learning?
- Why is it essential for you?
- Why is it so necessary on the study table?
- What personal emotions are attached to the object?

After group sharing, gather students in a circle and debrief:
- How certain things were more important than others?
- How things selected reflects how one learns and studies?
- What are essential factors in learning?
- Comment on how resources and materials are just tools for learning.
- What are various ways in which students in you class like to learn?

Skill and competencies Expected from students[5]
- Work collaboratively
- Read, analyze and synthesize information
- Present information coherently
- Articulate ideas orally and in writing
- Ask relevant question
- Take self-study approach
- Think critically

At this moment, brief students about learning and thinking and what is expected from students (hint above). In addition, sometime should be given to students to brainstorm their own expectations from the whole class.

Classroom Tips: Metaphors for learning

Following are some of the metaphors
- A candle shedding the darkness of ignorance
- Nutrition for a seed to grow into a tree
- A lock and a key
- A Window

Finally, involve students (in groups or individually) in drawing out their metaphor for learning and how they see themselves involved in the learning process from now on.

STORIES FROM LITERATURE

Students will be engaged in reflective learning through this video analysis exercise. **First**, play this video (www.youtube.com/watch?HgDWvLOodHw&t=55s) on the "Giving Tree".
While students are watching the clip ask students to note down their learning from the movie using the following Reflective Thinking Model[6].

> "If you talk to a man in a language he understands that goes to his head. If you talk to him in his own language, that goes to his heart.
>
> Nelson Mandela.

- *Description:*
    What did they see? What happened?
- *Interpretation:*
    Why did this happen?
- *Relevance:*
    How is it relevant today? What's in it for me?
- *Implication:*
    How can I apply the learning in my own experiences?
- *Query:*
    What was not clear? What do I need to know further?

Then, facilitate students, using the following prompts above) in thinking about ways in which human beings learn. Observations, personalization, reflection and sharing of knowledge are amongst the ways. Emphasize on using the reflective thinking model in each class from now on and in their everyday lives to facilitate learning.

- How does the boy learning?
- What elements is he using to help him?
- How?
- What makes human learn from others?
    What are the processes involve in learning?
- How can you learn and progress?

Finally, ask students to practice reflective thinking by creating 'Object stories'. Ask students to bring in any object or imagine any object (while a soft music is being played) that they think is most attached to their own lives. Engage them in writing down their reflective pieces of writing using the above format (description, interpretation, query, relevance and implication).

Sample Reflective Writing Piece[7]

Challis Nicole Clelland Part 1. *This week in interpersonal (week 1) we were instructed to get to know our classmates; we played with a toy ball that we threw to each other to remember everyone's names. The self-assessment, a paper where we judge how we communicate and who we communicate best with, was very helpful to me; it help me learn more about myself. When we were divided into groups and told to make a list of rules, creatively; I became ecstatic and got to know my classmates even better! Even in break I was invited /included to spend time with my group in the common area, but because I am a little hesitant when meeting new people and like to keep my distance, and declined. After break we finished our norm poster and presented them, our group called ours "We Got Your Back" meaning that our class will stick up for each other. I feel that we learned a lot in just three hours and am excited to see what the semester brings.*

October 7, 2011 at 11:24 am

Classroom Tips: Looking at objects[8]

- Look carefully at the objects
- Describe what you see, hear, touch, feel and smell
- Infer what these feelings/thoughts mean
- Look at the whole object (from various angles and perspectives) or parts of it to be specific
- Be specific- use the details to interpret its relevance with your own lives.
- Use your own prior experiences and knowledge

Students may be as creative as they want to be in order to present their reflective pieces. It may be a writing piece, poem, artwork or a presentation.

I AM HUMAN NATION

This exercise will encourage students to acknowledge humans as intellectual being. **First**, lead students to fill following table about brain and its functions individually for few minutes (see below for reference).

> "He who questions much does and discusses much, shall learn much."
>
> Sir Francis Bacon

After that, divide them into groups of four and facilitate them to compare their tables with those done by others in the class and reflect:
- Why do they presented their respected views?
- Why do they believe what they believe about brain?
- How various opinions are different or similar to one another?
- What are the other facts they know about brain, intellect and creation of human beings?

	Claims[9]	Yes	No	Not sure
1	Brains are like car engines. You have to look after them otherwise they will break down.			
2	There is no limit to what the human brain can do.			
3	There is nothing in your brain when you are born.			
4	Girls' brains work faster than boys' brains.			
5	Brain is just a computer			
6	Most people only ever use a tiny part of their brain.			

Then, engage students (in groups or individually) in analyzing the image (see below for reference) and answer the following questions.
- How do you think people opinion about brain, intellect and mind shapes the way they work and behave in this world?
- Which of the opinion is most appealing and relevant for you? Give reasons.

Finally, divide students in groups of three and ask them to construct their own metaphor for brain and its functions and create a reflective poem about it. Following questions may be of some guidance
- How they picture their brain works?
- How brain functions as compared with other objects? How complex it is?
- How it is used by humans in getting various jobs done?

Sample Poem[10]

Hope (by Emily Dickinson)

Hope is the thing with feathers
That perches in the soul
And sings the tune
Without the words
And never stops at all.

And sweetest in the gale is heard;
And sore must be the storm that could abash the little bird
That kept so many warm

I've heard it in the chilliest land,
And on the strangest sea;
Yet, never, in extremity,
It asked a crumbed of me.

Classroom Tips: Group discussions[11]

- <u>Create:</u> What is your idea? What do you think about?
- <u>Clarify:</u> Ask clarifying questions. What does that mean? Say more about... can you elaborate...
- <u>Negotiate:</u> Where do you agree or disagree? How your ideas are similar or different?
- <u>Fortify:</u> How do you support your idea? What is the example?

A: My brain is like a huge hotel with millions of rooms. Each room is full of things I've learned.

B: I think my brain is like a computer, but slower. I work things out carefully, step by step.

C: I always get in a muddle when I've got a hard problem to think about. My brain is like a pan of spaghetti.

D: My brain is like an anthill, with millions of tiny passageways. There is always something going on in my head. The ants never seem to rest.

E: My brain is like a naughty puppy! It never does what I want it to do. If I've got Maths homework to do it wants to read a comic or watch television.

F: My brain is like a massive forest. It's full of amazing ideas. But some of these ideas are like shy animals, they hide away in the middle of the forest. I don't think we can really understand how our brains work.

Which people said something positive (good) about brain?
Which people said something negative (bad) about their brain?
Who do you think might be good at creative things like writing stories and songs? Why?
Who do you think would be best at working out practical problems? Why?

MOST PRECIOUS GIFT FROM GOD[12]

To appreciate the gift of God – time, following exercise is suggested. **First,** divide the class into teams of 4 and provide each team with a stopwatch. Each member of the team will be assigned following roles and will be asked to perform respective tasks on their turns.

"Time is the only resource that everyone has the same amount of. No two people use their time the same way. What you do with your time shows what you think is important."

Anonymous

1. Silent observer
2. Problem solver
3. Sports person
4. Active Reader

Ask each member of the team to perform their task on their turn while counting for a minute to pass. With the start alert, team will set their stopwatch on and assigned person will begin their allotted task. As soon as the individual thinks that a minute has passed, he/she would call 'stop' and team members will record/note the time from the stopwatch. This exercise will continue in 4 rounds till each member completes their turn.

During each round, the assigned member of the team will be completing the task while noting for a minute to pass, while others members will try and keep him/her from counting the seconds. **In the end**, task vs time chart will be compiled in each groups and compared with others in the class.

Sample Calculations

	Students of grade 8	Average Life span	Remaining
Years	13	70	57
Days (x365)	4745	25550	20805
Hours (x24)	113880	613200	499320
Minutes (x60)	6832800	36792000	29959200
Seconds (x60)	409968000	2207520000	1797552000

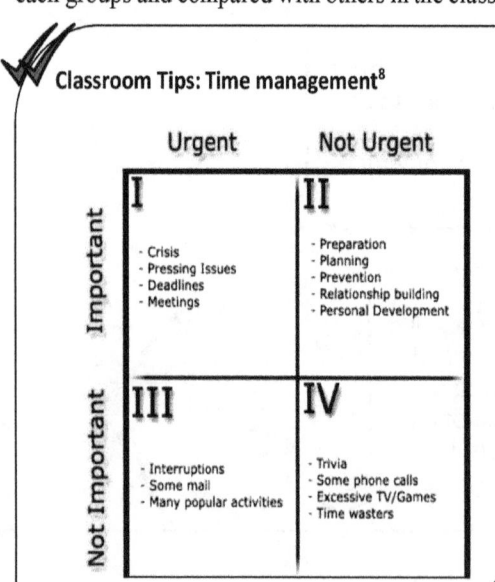

Classroom Tips: Time management[8]

Then, discuss the findings.
- Identify times when minute seem to pass quickly or slowly.
- What factors make you think time has passed quickly or slowly?
- How cautious were you with every passing time?
- How you prioritize/ spend time in your daily lives?
- List ways you think time is wasted?

In addition, teacher can engage students in some calculations regarding days, hours, minutes and seconds passed of their own lives. How much time is still left if average life span is 70yrs?

Finally, involve students in writing a reflection about ways in which they spend their time? How can they use their time effectively to meet their needs and wants? How they can save time? How they can invest constructively in their lives by consciously utilizing their time?

READING PICTURES[14]

This strategy is suggested to assist students to be able to analyze and read picture closely. **First,** divide students into pairs. Give one person in the pair an image and ask them to start describing the image to the other person.
- What is the place?
- Who are these people?
- What are they doing?
- What is going on in the image?
- Who is doing what and where? And so on.

> "An image is that which presents an intellectual and emotional complex in an instant of time."
>
> Ezra Pound

While the partner describes the image, another will draw the description based on what he listens.

After they have finished their description and drawing, facilitate them to compare their images. What differences and similarities they observe? How are their drawings specific to description of image? What could have been better description for the image? How would you describe/draw differently?

Then, together in pairs, ask students to list down top 15 things they see people doing in the image (each on separate piece of paper) and try to think of a motive (the reasons why they do things) for each of the actions.

Sample actions[14]
1. A woman walking up and down the platform.
2. A man tying a small girl's scarf.
3. A guard going into the Staff Office.
4. A girl bursting into tears.
5. Two people unpacking their rucksacks.
6. A porter running after three children.
7. A Policeman standing in a doorway.
8. Two people singing
9. A woman photographing the rails.
10. A teenager sticking a postage stamp onto the platform.

Let students to imagine tales behind people actions in the image - why people are doing what they are doing at the station? And compare their responses with others in the class and discuss
- Why their responses differ from each other?
- What leads to these responses?

Finally, lead students to think about their own-selves at the station and write a written reflection using the following prompt
What they think they will be doing (traveler, passersby, waiting and so on) and why if they will be at the station?
- What are your interests?
- How you behave in certain situations?
- How you interact with others?

Classroom Tips: Reading pictures[15]

- List everything you see in the picture. What was your eye drawn to first and why?
- Identify shapes, patterns and characters. How are the details arranged in the picture?
- Find the detail that stands out. What in the picture or in your own experience made this detail stand out?
- Find the connection, relationship between objects/characters. What story is being told? What has already happened?

STEADFASTNESS ON BELIEFS[16]:

For students to realize pressures one faces in this world in keeping them focused following exercise has been organized. **First,** divide students into two equal groups and let them stand facing each other. Students from each team (those standing at one end of the line) will be asked to take a walk between the lines from their end to the other extreme without smiling. People standing at each side may try to make the opposing team member smile by passing on reasonable comments, sharing jokes, making funny faces and so on; but DO NOT TOUCH THEM.

> "When you find yourself on the side of the majority, you should pause and reflect."
>
> Mark Twain

Those members of the team, who manage to pass the line without smiling will join their own teams at the other end; while those who let themselves loose and smile will join the opposing team. Task is to get maximum team members on your side by making opposing team members smile or at least keep the original members intact.

After all pairs have passed through the line, ask them to reflect:
- How were you feeling when it was your turn to walk between the lines?
- How different were the feelings when you were standing on the sidelines and when were you walking in between the lines?
- How did your group manage through the task?
- How does this activity relate to personal situations?

Now, give students another change to play the game again in their original groups. But this time, additional time would be given to plan or strategize their team's move for the game.

Then, facilitate students' discussion using following questions:
- How was the experience different?
- What new strategies you thought for the game?
- How does this activity relate to personal situations?
- How important it is to remain focus on what's important for you?
- How does it make you feel?

Finally, ask students to complete the following phrases about their own selves. Ask them to reflect in writing what three things they will now say 'no' or 'yes' to at least for a week using the following guidelines.

I know that ... because ... but I will try ...

I enjoy ... as I like ... but I know that ...

I don't ... for I ... but from now on it is my duty to ...

I am not ... because ... but I can always ...

Classroom Tips: Playing a game

- Divide teams randomly or with appropriate scheme to avoid mess
- Make instructions loud and clear.
- Give teams some time for settlement and ask clarifying questions (if any) before the game
- Set up game time and stick by it
- Chose a attention grabbing signal that all students must recognize
- Close the game properly to direct students' attention back

Sense of Responsibility[21]

Living in this world means that there are rights, duties and responsibilities. Fulfilment of responsibilities as an obligation shows how much one is dutiful. People around you expect you to do things because they are due or ought to be done. This willing obedience is dutifulness and shows how much your sense of responsibility makes you committed or devoted to this value. It also shows your humble, submissive, polite and obedient nature.

END OF A DEDICATED CAREER

An elderly carpenter was ready to retire. He told his boss of his plans to leave and live a more leisurely life. The contractor was sorry to see such a good worker go, and he asked the Carpenter to build just one more house as a personal favour. The Carpenter agreed but in time it was easy to see that his heart was not in his work. He resorted to shoddy workmanship and used inferior material. It was an unfortunate way to end a dedicated career.

When the Carpenter finished the work, his contractor came to inspect the house. He handed the keys to Carpenter; "This is your house." The contractor said, "It is my gift to you" The Carpenter was shocked. If he had known he was building his own house, he would have done it differently.

This story tells us that we should do everything with a dedicated sense of responsibility.

This quality should become a part of education and upbringing. When the youth realize the importance of being dutiful, they affect the entire surroundings. A family becomes strong as a unit; a community benefits largely in its development and ultimately a whole nation progresses as this individual quality combines collectively to express solidarity and strength.

If a nation is left behind on the path of progress, development and well-being, it means that its people are not motivated by a sense of responsibility. No doubt you have rights in the society you live, but every right implies a responsibility; every opportunity you come across has an obligation. The more this society and nation gives us, the more dutiful we have to be.

HUMAN SQUARES

For team building and leadership experience, **First,** divide students in groups of 4s or 8s. Blindfold everyone in the group. Challenge the group to position themselves within their groups to form a square.

Give students ample time to think, plan and execute their human squares while they are blindfold. Once the group thinks that they have created a square, allow everyone to take off their blindfolds and to look at what shape they actually have created.

"One learns by doing the thing; for though you think you know it, you have no certainty until you try."

Sophocles

Facilitate the post-activity discussion using following questions.
- What happened during this activity?
- What went well?
- If you are given the chance to play this again in a group, what would you do differently?
- What did you learn from this game?
- What did you learn about yourself? About teams?

Then ask each student to think about how teams are formed? Involve them in developing the ladder for team building (from individual to formation of team) using the given format and hint

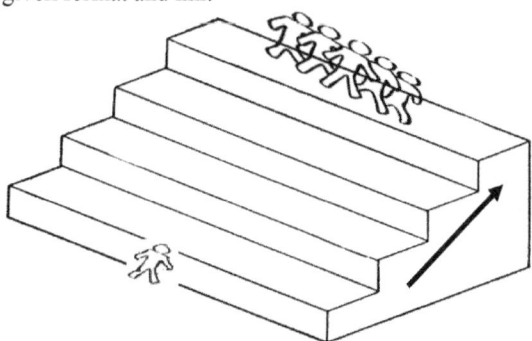

Finally, ask them to design a poster about motivating an existing or imaginary team using the following guidelines
- How teams are effective for work?
- What motivates people to work together?
- What benefits are offered in teams?
- What will be your tagline?
- How will you support your teammates?

What Makes a Team

Members want or choose to be part of the team and are proud of their membership
Members share a common vision and goal
Members are comfortable sharing duties because they know they can count on others
Members trust others to do what they say they will because they're committed to the team
Members trust their leader
Trust is important to members so the team can continue to succeed
Members are valued for what they bring to the team and their talents are used to strengthen the team; they're interested in how they can interact with one another
Members know their leader is comfortable asking them for help or to take on a leadership role if necessary
Members are active and look for opportunities to move forward; they want to examine how decisions are made and put into action
Members see conflict and mistakes as opportunities to learn and grow
Members realize their power and influence as individuals and as a team

---

Classroom Tips: Building a Team[22]

<u>Build commitment</u>: Clearly express what you expect and why?
<u>Instill confidence</u>: Recognize what individual members bring to the team.
<u>Inspire trust</u> Act responsible, do as promised and keep committed
<u>Empower others:</u> enabling your team successfully to do it themselves.

MEANING MAKING[23]

In this strategy, students learn to make relevant notes or highlight key elements from the text while they read and use separate colors to mark each category for better understanding of the text.

"Books without connection to knowledge of life are useless ... for what should books teach but the art of living?"

Sameul Johnson

First, model this reading exercise with students using the text Lead students to highlight the following elements using various color codes and record their responses in the separate sheet of paper as they read

- *Questions: Blue*
    What is not clear from the text? What I need to know more about? Who is what in the text?
- *Vocabulary: Red*
    Any difficult words from the text. Any phrase/word meaning that is not clear or does not make sense.
- *Claims: Yellow*
    Any universal truths, scientific claims, researched outcomes, key opinions from the text, viewpoints of author.
- *Supporting evidences: Green*
    What evidences or examples are used to support the claims highlighted above? Any facts added to support the claim
- *Connections: Orange*
    How this text is relevant to what you already know? To the world around? To you? How does it connect to other texts you have read or come across?

Summarizing a text
- Start with pulling out the main idea
- Use key words and phrases that support the main idea
- Present ideas logically and clearly
- Close your writing appropriately
- Use your own words

Now, engage students in discussion using following questions:
  -How they understood the text?
  -What connections and relevance they can draw from the text while reading it?
  -How do these color codes help them in understanding the text better?
  -What will they do next time while reading and analyzing the text?

Then, ask them to practice the close reading skill in groups or individually with other text following teacher modelling done at the beginning.

Finally, ask students to use the highlighted key words, opinions or any connections marked or noted down into a cohesive summary. Encourage students to use their own words and connections to rewrite their pieces.

Classroom Tips: Close Reading

Instead of using colors, students may use pencil marks onto the text to highlight the above elements

➢ Ask student to read the text twice
➢ Get the gist of what the text is about. Mark a star on key points
➢ Circle difficult words
➢ Place a question mark (?) to raise a question or answer questions raised
➢ Make connections from the text (use the left column to write)
➢ Use numbers to list down examples / evidences / claims
➢ Read again to summarize

THE NEXT STOP:

In this task, students are involved in video prediction and analyses technique. Video titled 'strawberries' is to be used for the task and they will be asked to reflect using the format below.

"Actions speaks louder than words, so believe what you see and forget what you heard."

Anonymous

Strawberry story is just an example you can use another story.

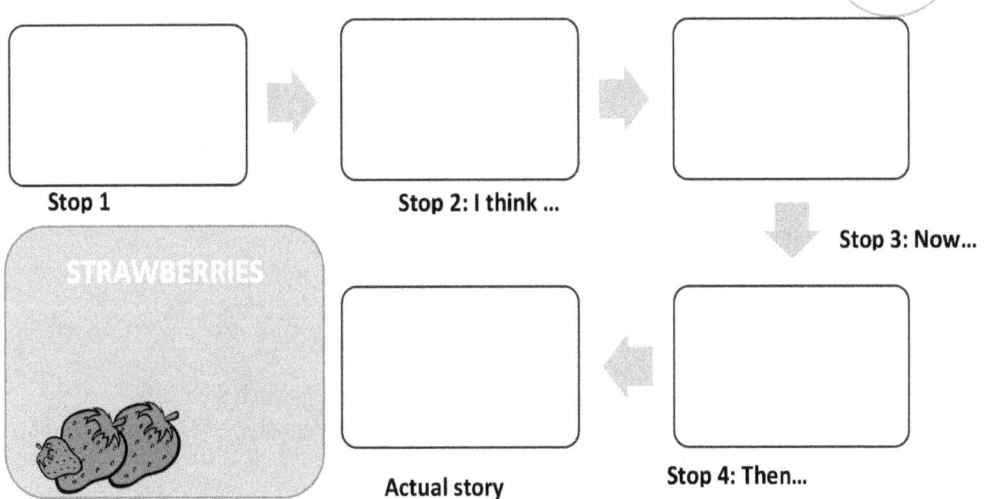

First, let students see the title of the video and let them imagine what would be in the video about and write in the first box. **Then** after few intervals (at 1:09m; 1.50m; 2.50m; 3.58m) teacher will pause the video and ask students to predict what will happen next. Give students ample time in between intervals to predict, imagine and write their stories in the given space.

After students have watched the video completely, then facilitate the discussion through following questions:
- How your predictions were similar to and different from the original video?
- What lead you to predict what you predicted?
- How each of the predictions is different?
- What lessons or essential elements can we learn from the video?

Finally, ask students to create a 'gratitude card/momento' for this girl who acted out of her wish to help the poor. What would you like to present this girl (and people similar to them in your own lives) so as to show appreciation towards their acts of kindness?

Classroom Tips: video prediction[24]

- Notice, observe, and envision key details about the character, setting and situations.
- Combine details to make connections and possible events to follow
- Use your previous experiences and knowledge to guide you.
- Use visual details to help you think, interpret and predict meanings and associations

INTELLECT IN ACTION

Reading fulfills its charm when it is shared and discussed with others. For practicing this skill, **first,** divide the whole class into two groups. One group will be arranged in an inner outward-facing circle and the other outer circle facing-inwards. Students facing outwards (inner circle) will be asked to compose a question (at least one) after surveying/skimming the given text (attached) and write these questions on a sheet of paper in front of them. Meanwhile, group facing inward (the outer circle) will actually be spending time in reading the given text.

> "Don't just teach your children to read... teach them to question what they read. Teach them to question everything."
>
> George Carlin

After the given time, students in the inner circle will ask their respective questions to the student in front of them (members of the outer circle) and get their responses. After 2-3 minutes inner circle may rotate clockwise and do the similar exercise with other members of the outer circle until the circle is complete.

Students in the inner circle, will be writing possible answers on the sheets of paper based on their conversation with the outer group and try and understand the text given.

After first round is complete, the groups may switch their roles and tasks and repeat the similar exercise with another reading text (attached).

Then, provide all students a silent reading time for students to go through the given texts and ask discuss their own understanding with others around the circle. Students may refer back to their questions and responses to them.

Teacher may lead the discussion if needed using the following guided questions:
- What were your understanding based on just skimming the text?
- How questions and paired discussions helped you in understanding the text?
- After reading the text yourself, what new things you learnt?
- How each text may be understood differently by different people?

Finally, students may be asked to work in their chosen pairs and write down their reflective dialogue about any one of the reading text using the following guidelines.

- What was A's questions?
- How did B responded to it?
- What A learns about the question from others in the circle?
- How does B respond to the question now?
- After reading, how A's views changed? Built upon? Or remained same?
- What were the shared learning?

Classroom Tips: Pre-reading texts[25]

Skim or survey through text title, subheadings, the table of contents, name of the author, opening paragraph, images or key points and ask questions like:
- What does this word mean in the text?
- What is the author key idea?
- What might be the purpose of writing this text?
- What characters are involved in the text?
- Why do I read it?
- How is it relevant?

Self-improvement and Growth[27]

Self-improvement is a process of self-growth which everyone, especially youngsters should adopt. It is not enough to read, you have to practise what you read and this needs your time and effort. There is no such thing as instant self-improvement. Any inner change takes time, and there must be motivation, desire, perseverance and dedication. Usually old habits do not allow us to bring about this change. There is also resistance and opposition from the people around us. The will to change has to overcome this opposition. One way of bringing a change in attitude and behaviour is to observe how people behave and act in different situations and then looking inside to find out if you would have behaved in the same way under similar circumstances. The positive traits of character in such situations should be adopted. In this way you learn and benefit a lot from the behaviour and actions of the people around you, in school, at home, in the street and everywhere else. It is not a matter of judging others, but learning how to act, react and behave in a better way. It will also increase your knowledge about how the mind and thoughts influence behaviour and action. If you do not like what you are, analyze what and why you dislike and then analyze your own behaviour in the same way. Similarly adopt this norm in character traits of others you like.

PUT THE GLASS DOWN!

A professor began his class by holding up a glass with some water in it. He held it up for all to see and asked the students, "How much do you think this glass weighs?"

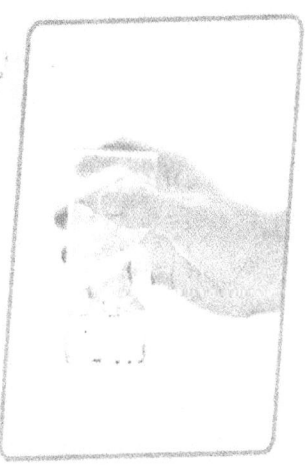

"50 grams... 100 grams... 125 grams..." the students answered. "I really don't know unless I weigh it," said the professor, but, my question is, "What would happen if I held it up like this for a few minutes?"

"Nothing!" the students replied. "Okay! What would happen if I held it up like this for an hour?" the professor asked. ""Your arm would begin to ache," said one of the students. "You're right! Now what would happen if I held it for a day?"

"Your arm could go numb; you might have severe muscle stress and paralysis, and have to go to hospital for sure!" ventured another student; and all the students laughed. "Very good! But during all this, did the weight of the glass change?" asked the professor. "No," the students replied. "Then what caused the arm ache and the muscle stress?"

The students were puzzled. "Put the glass down," said one of the students. "Exactly!" said the professor, "Life's problems are something like this. Hold it for a few minutes in your head and they seem okay. Think of them for a long time and they begin to ache. Hold it even longer and they begin to paralyse you. You will not be able to do anything."

The Moral: My dear friends, it's important to think of the challenges (problems) in our life, but even more important is to 'put them down' at the end of every day before we go to sleep. That way, we are not stressed and wake up every day fresh and strong and can handle any issue, any challenge that comes our way. Remember to 'PUT THE GLASS DOWN' and have tranquillity by putting trust in your abilities and finding solutions to problems that come your way. It is no use wasting your time in lingering over problems that can only go away when a proper solution is worked out.

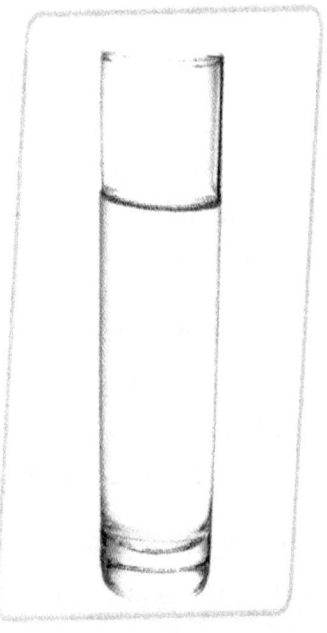

MY UNIQUE PERSPECTIVE

This activity is designed to understand individual viewpoint. **At the beginning of the class,** teacher take one toy egg (or an oval piece) in class and nominate one student as a caretaker for that imaginary egg. During the class whatever that child do and wherever he go he should take that egg with him/her.

> "What you see depends not only what you look at, but also on where you look from."
>
> James Deacon

Then, divide students into 4 groups representing following people
- Poultry Farmer
- Hungry person
- Person like to eat egg everyday
- Trader for egg in an international market

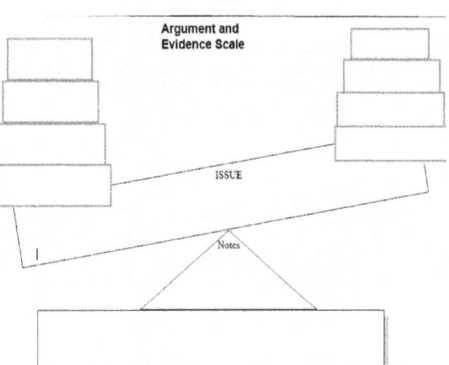

Give students time to brainstorm their arguments about how valuable that egg is for them. Facilitate students to list down supporting statements regarding why that egg should be given to them.

Teacher may prompt that an egg that has been brought to the class will be given to the group who will present best arguments in support or against rewarding the egg to their group rather than the other.

Now, jumble up students in pairs (each pair formed with 2 individual from different group) and ask them to engage in argumentative dialogue about who should be the rightful receiver of the egg. Students may use argument scale to weigh each other's points[28] (each member may add arguments in favor of their role on the scale and those whose scale lean will win the debate).

After, sufficient discussion time, involve students in an whole group reflection using following questions
- What were your individual arguments based on?
- Who was winning the argument? And why?
- How each group was valuing the egg differently?
- Who was more sensitive towards the egg than others?

While discussing with students, deliberately take the egg from the egg-keeper and symbolically break it on the floor. Note students' reactions for few minutes and then involve them in discussion again:
- How did you feel now that the egg is broken?
- Now that the egg is broken, does it make any difference to your whole argumentative discussion earlier?
- What is more valuable? an egg? Or people?
- How people create perspective about things that can just be temporary?
- How can this dilemma be avoided?

> **Classroom Tips: Group discussions**[28]
>
> - <u>Create</u>: What is your idea? What do you think about?
> - <u>Clarify</u>: Ask clarifying questions. What does that mean? Say more about... can you elaborate...
> - <u>Negotiate</u>: Where do you agree or disagree? How your ideas are similar or different?
> - <u>Fortify</u>: How do you support your idea? What is the example?

Finally, ask students to write a reflective piece about any similar experience that might have occurred in their lives where they had to face contrasting perspectives.

INFORMED DECISIONS[29]

For students to analyze information effectively, following activity is formulated. **First,** ask students to bring various print ads from a newspaper or magazine or the teacher may bring some for the class to work on.

Engage students in analyzing the ad using following questions on a separate sheet of paper.
- What does the ad say or suggest about the product or service?
- What is the ad trying to make you buy, think or do?
- What audience is the ad targeting? What makes you think so?
- What techniques does the ad use?
- What does the ad say about the people who buy the product or service?
- How one can be aware of the product truths and lies?
- What should a person believe in while buying a product?

Now, divide students in groups and provide them some time to create special products for the following phrases and perform ads for their products in front of the whole class.

- Smile is the best form of charity
- Humans are mortal beings
- A new year's resolution
- A friend in need is a friend indeed
- Spread happiness and reduce sadness

Students may keep in mind
- What are the characteristic of the product?
- What marketing strategy they will be suing?
- What will be their tagline?
- How would they influence people to buy their product?

> "Learn everything you can, anytime you can, from anyone you can; there will always come a time when you will be grateful you did."
>
> Sarah Caldwell

Sample Ad Techniques

Association: using images in the hope that it will increase sales (like a cartoon character)
Call to action: telling you what to do (Like buy now!)
Claim: informing you about how products works or helps you
Humor: using ads to make you laugh.
Hype: using words to make product exciting (like amazing, incredible, super)
Fear: using a product to solve something you worry about (like yellow teach)
Prizes and gifts: using a chance to win prize for attraction
Repetition: repeating a message or idea so you remember it.
Sales and price: announcing a discounted price
Sense appeal: using images and sounds to appeal your senses (like, taste, sight, tough)
Product Specialty: promoting a special ingredient that makes product different from others
Endorsements: featuring celebrities saying how product worked for them.

Finally, ask students to complete their written reflection using the following prompt:
How one can make informed decisions and motivates others to work constructively for the society in this distorted world?

Classroom Tips: Making an Ad

<u>Target Audience:</u> who do you think are the potential buyers or users of your product?
<u>Target market:</u> where would you sell your product to get to the target audience?
<u>Research:</u> what do you know about your target audience and market? Survey or interview
<u>Technique:</u> which technique you would use for your ad?
<u>Medium:</u> which medium would you choose to place your ad? Newspaper or internet or TV
<u>Create:</u> based on the information create your ad. What images, colors and texts would you use?

THE FINAL DAY

All of the class will be involved in creating a final day remembrance mural. Students will be involved in creating their classroom mural as reflective of their key moments and learning during the term.

"Give the pupils something to do, not something to learn; and the doing is of such a nature as to demand thinking; learning naturally results. ."

John Dewey

First, let students go back in time and reflect on the whole term and try to recall any best moment in the class or any key learning from various activities performed in the class, some insightful experiences that triggered them inside out or any feelings they want to express on to the collective piece of art. Their reflective journal or portfolio will assist them in thinking and selection. **Then,** facilitate each student to come up with a symbolic representation of their experiences from the classroom and present it into a collective class Mural.

Following process can be used in order to create a mural:

Sample Reflective Artwork[30]

- Decide the canvas on which to create a collective piece of art or Mural (a cloth, a large chart sheet, or small papers later joined together into a collage)
- Discuss with students how they want their Mural or collage to look like as a whole.
- Ask each student to bring in their own idea or key learning metaphor for the larger picture
- Collaborate, share and motivate each students to contribute something for the final work
- Exhibit your collaborative art work for others to see.

Classroom Tips: reflective questions

Reflective writing involves a process of self-assessment that can be meaningful and memorable

- What happened? What went well? What was most challenging?
- How were you involved?
- How does it make you feel?
- What did I learn about collaborating with a group?
- What did I learn about myself?
- How should one engage in discussion?
- What were some new and exciting occurring during the term?
- What would you do differently from now on to involve in the learning process?
- Were your expectations met?
- How you see yourself grow during the course of time?

References:

1. CBM. 2010. Competency based Module. STEP Cohort 1. ITREB for India

2. Paul, Fisher and Noish, 1993, p.4 in Fisher, Alec. 2001. Critical Thinking, An Introduction. Cambridge University Press.

3. McCarty, T., Watahomigie, L. J., Perez, B., Torres-Guzman, M. E. 2004. Sociocultural Contexts of Language and Literacy. Taylor & Francis. Pg. 26, 35

4. Kostelnik, M., Whiren, A., Soderman, A., Rupiper, M., Gregory, K. 2014. Guiding Children's Social Development and Learning. Cengage Learning. pg. 2, 4.

5. IIS, 2010. One World Many Hopes. Ethical Pathways to Human Developments. Skills and competencies. Islamic publication limited. Pg. 9

6. Wilhelm, J. D. 2007. Engaging Readers & Writers with inquiry. Scholastic. USA

7. Clelland, C. N. 2012. Reflective writing piece. as retrieved on August 30, 2014; https://usergeneratededucation.wordpress.com/tag/reflection/

8. Wilhelm, J. D. 2004. Reading is Seeing. Scholastic USA

9. Adapted from: Culshaw Chris & Craig David. 1990. Headwork 5. Oxford University Press.

10. Moustaki, Nikki. 2001. Writing poetry. The complete idiot's guide to writing poetry. Alpha books. USA

11. Zwiers, O'Hara, & Pritchard. 2014. *Common Core Standards in diverse classrooms: Essential practices for developing academic language and disciplinary literacy*. Adapted from the online course module on conversational tools by Novoed.com

12. Adapted from: Carpenter, Z. L. Texas Agricultural Extension service. The Texas A&M University System. College Station, Texas.

13. Covey, S. R. 2004. 7 Habits of Highly Effective People. Time management matrix.

14. Adapted from: Culshaw Chris & Craig David. 1990. Headwork 5. Oxford University Press.

15. Wilhelm, J. D. 2004. Reading is Seeing. Scholastic USA

16. Culshaw Chris & Craig David. 1990. Headwork 5. Oxford University Press.

17. Culshaw Chris & Craig David. 1990. Headwork 5. Oxford University Press.

18. MacGregor, M. G. 2007. Teambuilding with Teens: Activities for Leadership, Decision Making, and Group Success. Free Spirit publishing

19. Wilhelm, J. D. 2004. Reading is Seeing. Scholastic USA

20. Interim curriculum II. ITREB, P.

21. Rafi, M. 2013. Moral Pathways for all ages. Paramount Publishing Enterprise. Pakistan Edition

22. MacGregor, M. G. 2007. Teambuilding with Teens: Activities for Leadership, Decision Making, and Group Success. Free Spirit publishing

23. Adapted from PACC. 2014. Teaching Miracles. Teaching module for Lead Language Educators Program in collaboration with AKESP.

24. Wilhelm, J. D. 2004. Reading is Seeing. Scholastic USA

25. Wilhelm, J. D. 2007. Engaging Readers & Writers with inquiry. Scholastic. USA

26. Interim Curriculum II, ITREB, O.

27. Rafi, M. 2013. Moral Pathways for all ages. Paramount Publishing Enterprise. Pakistan Edition

28. Zwiers, O'Hara, & Pritchard. 2014. *Common Core Standards in diverse classrooms: Essential practices for developing academic language and disciplinary literacy.* Adapted from the online course module on conversational tools by Novoed.com

29. Admongo. N.d. Federal Trade Commission. Admongo.gov. grade 5-6. As retrieved on August 30, 2014; http://www.admongo.gov/_pdf/curriculum/FTC-Lesson-Plans-Student-Worksheets.pdf

30. Nathani, A. 2014. Coursework submission. Visitor Management. Museum studies. The University of Queensland Australia. Unpublished assignment

31. Silverstein, Shel. "The Giving Tree". YouTube, uploaded by Custom and Craft, 10 February 2017,(www.youtube.com/watch?HgDWvLOodHw&t=55s)

Other Referred sources:

Kemper, D., Meyer, V., Rys, J. V., Sebranek, P. 2012. Fusion: Integrated Reading and Writing, Book 2. Cengage learning

Sugar, S. (2002). *Primary Games: Experiential Learning Activities for Teaching Children K-8.* San Francisco: Jossey-Bass.

WEST, R. L., & TURNER, L. H. (2009). *Understanding interpersonal communication: making choices in changing times.* Boston, Thomson/Wadsworth.

Publishing by: Maple Leaf Publishing Inc.
3rd Floor 4915 54 Street
Red Deer, Alberta T4N 2G7, Canada

www.mapleleafpublishinginc.com

To order additional copies of this book, contact:
+1 (403) 356-0255

Paperback: **978-1-77419-019-7**
E-book: **978-1-77419-030-2**

www.ingramcontent.com/pod-product-compliance
Lightning Source LLC
Chambersburg PA
CBHW081423080526
44589CB00016B/2647